LET'S WORK IT OUT™

WITHDRAWN

How to deal with FEELING LEFT OUT

Rachel Lynette

PowerKiDS press™

New York

Published in 2009 by The Rosen Publishing Group, Inc.
29 East 21st Street, New York, NY 10010

First Edition

Editor: Joanne Randolph
Book Design: Kate Laczynski
Photo Researcher: Jessica Gerweck

Photo Credits: Cover, p. 1 © Yellow Dog Productions/Getty Images; p. 4 © Alistair Berg/Getty Images; pp. 6, 8 Shutterstock.com; p. 10 © Adrian Samson/Getty Images; p. 12 © David Deas/Getty Images; p. 14 © Elyse Lewin/Getty Images; p. 16 © Superstudio/Getty Images; p. 18 © Nicholas Prior/Getty Images; p. 20 © Baerbel Schmidt/Getty Images.

Library of Congress Cataloging-in-Publication Data

Lynette, Rachel.
    How to deal with feeling left out / Rachel Lynette. — 1st ed.
        p. cm. — (Let's work it out)
    Includes index.
    ISBN 978-1-4042-4520-4 (library binding)
    1. Social isolation—Juvenile literature. I. Title.
    HM1131.L96 2009
    155.4'18232—dc22
                                            2008009699

Manufactured in the United States of America

Contents

Tim's father coached Tim's sister's basketball team. Tim sometimes felt left out when his father spent so much time with his sister.

Feeling Left Out?

Emma, Lucy, and Julia always played together at recess. Then one day, Emma and Julia decided that they did not want to play with Lucy. Lucy's feelings were hurt. She did not understand why her friends had left her out.

Have you ever felt left out by your friends? No one likes to feel left out, but it happens to everyone sometimes. Feeling left out means that you feel that you are not being **included** in a group. When you feel left out, you may also feel sad, **confused**, and angry.

Bullies are often left out because they do not treat others well. Some bullies just do not know how to let others know they want to be part of the group.

Not Getting Along with Others

Sometimes, a person is left out because she does not get along well with others. Whenever Tiffany plays with other children, she bosses everyone else around and always wants to go first. Sometimes, she even cheats, or tricks people so she can win. Would you want to play with Tiffany?

A person may be left out because he has done something that hurt another person in the group. Tony called Ben a mean name. Now Ben and his friends do not want to play with Tony. Groups work well when everyone tries to get along with each other.

It can be hard to talk to other people when you are shy. If you make the first move, you will find that most people are happy to make a new friend.

Feeling Shy

Some people feel left out because they are shy. Kylie ate lunch alone every day. She wanted to eat with Nicole and Maria. Even though they seemed nice, Kylie was afraid to ask.

Shy people often want to be part of a group but are afraid to join in. They worry that the other kids will not like them. Shy people feel afraid of being **rejected**.

Often people in groups do not mean to **exclude** others. The group may not realize that another person would like to be included. Sometimes, you have to make the first move, even if you are shy.

It may feel like the people in a group do not want any more friends. You will never know unless you try to make friends with them, though.

Making the First Move

It can be hard to join a group, but there are some things you can do to make it easier. One thing that will help is to smile at people. Smiling lets people know that you are happy to be with them.

Next, talk to someone in the group. Try giving that person a **compliment** or asking her a question about what the group is doing. This lets people know that you are interested. Often, when you start talking to people in a group, you become part of the group without even having to ask!

People will not play with you if you always get upset when you lose a game. Learn how to work well with others, so you will not be left out.

Part of the Group

Part of being in a group is being **considerate** of other people in the group. Treat the other members of the group with respect.

If the group is playing a game, follow the rules. Be a good sport. Do not try to get everyone to do things your way. Instead of trying to stand out, pay attention to other people. Be yourself, but try to fit in, too. This will help people see that you are a good team player. Then, they will want you to be a part of their group.

Tory had wanted to join the drama club, but they told her it was too late. She knew that next year she would have to try out earlier.

When It Is Not You

Sometimes, other people will not let you join their group no matter how hard you try. You may think it is because of something you did. If you treated these people with kindness and respect, though, it likely was not because of you.

Sometimes, the timing just is not right. Maybe the group was playing a game, and there was no room for another player. Perhaps they did not want to stop to explain the rules. Maybe the group was talking about something **private**. It may help to remember that you are a good person. Try not to take this kind of rejection **personally**.

Jake used to hog the ball during basketball practice.
Soon, the other players did not pass him the ball
anymore, so he tried to be a better team player.

When It Is You

Sometimes, people will not let you join a group because they do not like you. What can you do to change their **opinions** of you? First, think about how you have treated other people in the group. Have you been mean or bossy? Have you had trouble sharing, waiting your turn, or following the rules?

It is hard to realize that you may not get along well with others. The good news is that you can change! Start treating other people the way that you would like to be treated. Play fairly. Be a good sport.

Sam felt bad when he was the last person picked for a team. When he talked to his dad, he found out that his dad used to get picked last, too.

Talk About Your Feelings

Being left out can really hurt your feelings. You may feel sad, lonely, and angry. It is important not to take your angry feelings out on other people, though. It may help to talk to an adult you trust, such as a **counselor**, teacher, or parent.

Learning to get along with others can take a long time. Sometimes, you will make mistakes, and that is okay. It may take a while for other people to notice that you have changed. Whenever you are with other people, remember to **cooperate** and treat everyone fairly. Soon you will be making friends and having fun!

Next time you see someone looking for a place to sit in the lunchroom, invite that person to sit at your table.

Leaving Others Out

Have you ever left someone else out of a group of which you are a part? You may have had a good reason. Perhaps that person is bossy or hard to get along with.

It may have seemed like a good idea to have left that person out. Try to remember that when you leave someone out, you hurt his feelings. Think about how you would feel if you were the one being left out. It can be hard to include people you do not like, but when you do, you help them learn how to get along with other people.

All Together!

What can you do to make sure no one feels left out? When you are in a group, make sure everyone is included. Look around, do you see anyone who is being left out? Ask that person to join in!

Everyone feels left out sometimes. When you feel left out, think about what you can do to change the **situation**. Do you need to make the first move and talk to someone? Do you need to change the way you treat people? Even a small change can make a big difference. Soon, you will be a part of the group, too!

Glossary

compliment (KOM-pluh-ment) Something good that is said about one.

confused (kun-FYOOZD) Mixed up.

considerate (kun-SIH-deh-rut) Treating other people fairly and not hurting people's feelings.

cooperate (koh-AH-per-ayt) To work with others.

counselor (KOWN-seh-ler) Someone who talks with people about their feelings and problems and who gives advice, or help.

exclude (eks-KLOOD) To keep someone out or shut out.

included (in-KLOOD-ed) Allowed to join in or be part of something.

opinions (uh-PIN-yunz) Beliefs that are based on what a person thinks rather than what is known to be true.

personally (PERS-nuh-lee) Feeling that something has to do with oneself.

private (PRY-vit) Keeping something to yourself.

rejected (rih-JEKT-ed) Not accepted.

situation (sih-choo-AY-shun) A problem or an event.

Index

Web Sites

Due to the changing nature of Internet links, PowerKids Press has developed an online list of Web sites related to the subject of this book. This site is updated regularly. Please use this link to access the list:
www.powerkidslinks.com/lwio/leftout/